For my fiancé Colin, as we embark
on life's greatest journey together — EC

GREAT
MIGRATIONS

A NATIONAL GEOGRAPHIC CHANNEL
GLOBAL TELEVISION EVENT

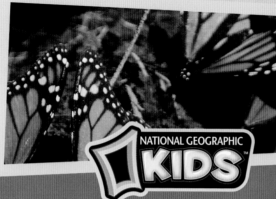

NATIONAL GEOGRAPHIC
KIDS

GREAT
MIGRATIONS

WHALES, WILDEBEESTS, BUTTERFLIES, ELEPHANTS, AND OTHER AMAZING ANIMALS ON THE MOVE

BY ELIZABETH CARNEY

NATIONAL GEOGRAPHIC
WASHINGTON, D.C.

GREAT MIGRATIONS
Shortest to Longest

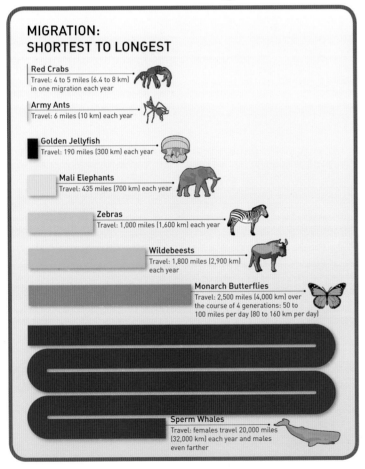

MIGRATION: SHORTEST TO LONGEST

Red Crabs
Travel: 4 to 5 miles (6.4 to 8 km) in one migration each year

Army Ants
Travel: 6 miles (10 km) each year

Golden Jellyfish
Travel: 190 miles (300 km) each year

Mali Elephants
Travel: 435 miles (700 km) each year

Zebras
Travel: 1,000 miles (1,600 km) each year

Wildebeests
Travel: 1,800 miles (2,900 km) each year

Monarch Butterflies
Travel: 2,500 miles (4,000 km) over the course of 4 generations: 50 to 100 miles per day (80 to 160 km per day)

Sperm Whales
Travel: females travel 20,000 miles (32,000 km) each year and males even farther

CONTENTS

INTRODUCTION 10

MALI ELEPHANTS 12

RED CRABS 16

BUTTERFLIES 20

JELLYFISH 24

ZEBRAS 28

ARMY ANTS 32

WILDEBEESTS 36

SPERM WHALES 40

INDEX 44

INTRODUCTION

ON AFRICA'S SERENGETI,

WILDEBEESTS FACE A TOOTHY TRIO—LIONS, HYENAS, AND CROCODILES—ANXIOUS TO EAT THEM. In North America, short-lived monarch

butterflies undertake such a long journey that it takes several generations

to complete the trip. On a remote tropical island, millions of crabs brave hordes of

acid-spraying ants in order to reach the sea and have their babies.

Animals migrate for a variety of reasons, some we know and some we don't.
They may need fresh sources of food or a place to mate. They might have to flee
from predators or find shelter from extreme temperatures. Each specific
migration featured here is based on filming from the National Geographic
Channel's global television event.

The sun—its rise and fall over a day and the whirling of the Earth around it
for a year—powers these events. They are some of nature's most thrilling
dramas. Come have a closer look at some of the world's great migrations.

☐ NATIONAL GEOGRAPHIC CHANNEL

GREAT MIGRATIONS

350 HOURS

PERCHED IN TREES
400 HOURS UNDERWATER;
150 HOURS IN
HELICOPTERS; 250 HOURS
FILMING AT NIGHT;
800 DAYS SHOOTING.

FILMED

EVERYWHERE
FROM THE SUB-ANTARCTIC
TO THE ARCTIC;
FROM THE SOUTH PACIFIC
TO THE
SAHARA TO SIBERIA.

MALI ELEPHANTS TO FIND ENOUGH FOOD AND WATER IN A VAST DESERT, FIVE-TON PACHYDERMS MUST DO A LOT OF WALKING.

DRIVEN BY THIRST

THERE'S A SAYING THAT AN ELEPHANT NEVER FORGETS.

For Mali desert elephants, that saying must be true. For them, forgetting the location of a lifesaving water hole would be a deadly mistake.

Mali elephants live along the southern edge of the Sahara desert. In order to survive in their parched environment, the animals are on a nearly constant search for water. A wise, older female, called a matriarch, leads each family group. The herd's survival depends on her decisions.

Under typical conditions, Mali elephants can thrive. But sometimes even the wisest matriarch is no match for nature. When a recent drought dried up nearly every water source in the region, the Malian government trucked in water for the elephants.

MALI ELEPHANTS FOLLOW A VAST COUNTER-CLOCKWISE CIRCLE THROUGH THE MALIAN SAHEL—A DESERT REGION SOUTH OF THE SAHARA.

THE ANIMALS TRAVEL OVER 435 (700 km) MILES EACH YEAR.

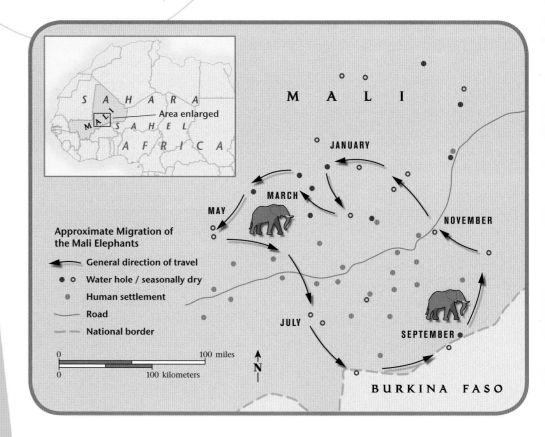

Approximate Migration of the Mali Elephants

➤ General direction of travel
● ○ Water hole / seasonally dry
● Human settlement
— Road
-- National border

0   100 miles
0   100 kilometers

N

MOTIVE TO MOVE:

MALI ELEPHANTS HAVE THE LONGEST MIGRATION OF ANY ELEPHANT. THEIR LIFE-OR-DEATH CHALLENGE IS TO FIND ENOUGH WATER IN A DESERT. AFTER A RARE RAIN, MALI ELEPHANTS MUST GET TO NEWLY-FORMED WATER HOLES BEFORE THEY DRY UP.

DANGERS:

OVEN-LIKE 120°F (49°C) HEAT AND FIERCE SAND STORMS CAN BE A DEADLY THREAT FOR TIRED, THIRSTY ELEPHANTS. YOUNGSTERS ARE THE MOST VULNERABLE.

ABOUT

400

ELEPHANTS PARTICIPATE IN THIS GREAT MIGRATION.

DIALING DUMBO

SCIENTISTS MONITOR THE MOVEMENTS OF MALI'S ELEPHANTS TO LEARN ABOUT THEIR NEEDS AND THE CHALLENGES THEY FACE. A conservation group called Save the Elephants tracks Mali elephants with high-tech GPS collars. The collars are linked to the Internet through a satellite phone network. Using hourly updates of elephant locations, scientists have mapped the elephants' migration with more detail than ever before.

RED CRABS

RED CRABS BLANKET THE GROUND ON CHRISTMAS ISLAND
DURING AN ANNUAL TREK TO THE BEACH TO MATE AND SPAWN.

EGG-MAKING MISSION

ON THE INDIAN OCEAN'S REMOTE CHRISTMAS ISLAND,

monsoon rains trigger the movement of a multitude. Millions of red crabs go on the march. They leave their forest burrows for a ten-day trek to the coast. Cherry-red crabs the size of dinner plates travel in a nearly straight line. They even go up and over obstacles—such as rocks, fallen branches, and roads—instead of around them. Their destination: the beaches where they were born. There they will mate and start a new generation of red crabs.

RED CRABS ARE THE RAIN FOREST'S **CLEANING CREW.** THEY EAT ANYTHING EDIBLE ON THE FOREST FLOOR. **NUTRIENTS** ARE RECYCLED **BACK** INTO THE SOIL THROUGH THE CRABS' DROPPINGS.

THE CRABS CRAWL A TOTAL OF 4 TO 5 MILES (6.5 to 8 km) **DURING THEIR JOURNEY TO AND FROM THE OCEAN.**

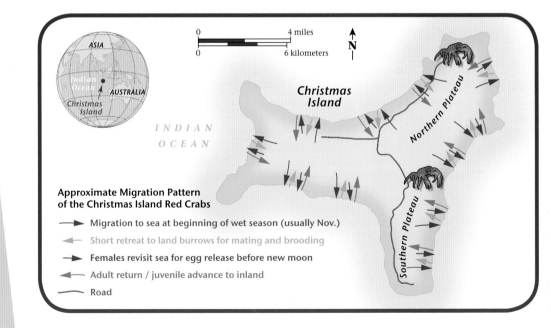

ASIA
Indian Ocean
AUSTRALIA
Christmas Island

INDIAN OCEAN

Christmas Island

Northern Plateau

Southern Plateau

0 — 4 miles
0 — 6 kilometers

N

Approximate Migration Pattern of the Christmas Island Red Crabs

→ Migration to sea at beginning of wet season (usually Nov.)
← Short retreat to land burrows for mating and brooding
→ Females revisit sea for egg release before new moon
← Adult return / juvenile advance to inland
— Road

MOTIVE TO MOVE:

ADULT RED CRABS ARE LAND DWELLERS, BUT THEIR EGGS MUST BE RELEASED IN THE OCEAN. MALES AND FEMALES CRAWL TO THE COAST IN SEPARATE SHIFTS. AFTER MATING, THE FEMALES LAY THEIR EGGS AND WAIT FOR A LOW TIDE. **THEN THEY BACKTRACK TO THEIR JUNGLE HOMES.**

DANGERS: BUSY ROADWAYS, LIMESTONE CLIFFS, AND TOO MUCH **SUN EXPOSURE** CAN ALL SEND CRABS TO THEIR DEATHS.

ABOUT **50** MILLION CRABS MAKE THIS **GREAT MIGRATION.**

CRAZY KILLERS

CRAZY ANTS ARE AN INVASIVE SPECIES ON CHRISTMAS ISLAND AND RED CRABS' TERRIFYING NEIGHBORS.

Ships accidentally brought the ants from West Africa in the 1970s. They quickly spread and now overwhelm the island's native creatures. Billions of ants have created "supercolonies" with more than 3,000 queens to a nest.

The fiercely territorial ants attack migrating crabs. Ants blind the crabs by spraying formic acid into their eyes. The disoriented crabs can't find shelter and dry out in the hot sun. Crazy ants have devastated the red crab population, cutting it in half during their forty years on the island.

BUTTERFLIES
MONARCH BUTTERFLIES TAKE FLIGHT FOR THE
LONGEST INSECT MIGRATION IN THE WORLD.

COLOR A-FLUTTER

IT'S SPRING IN MEXICO'S OYAMEL FORESTS. After

blanketing nearly every inch of the trees, millions of

monarch butterflies take flight. Their orange-and-black

wings color the sky like an explosion of confetti.

With the sun as their compass, they head north. No

one butterfly will live long enough to complete the entire

journey. Instead, they rely on a map imprinted in their

genes. Each new generation of butterfly picks up where its

parents left off. Together, they travel farther than

any known insect.

THE **BUTTERFLIES'** MIGRATION IS ONE OF THE **LONGEST** ON THE **PLANET** IN RELATION TO BODY SIZE. A MONARCH'S JOURNEY IS THE EQUIVALENT OF A PERSON CIRCLING THE EARTH 11 TIMES.

MONARCHS TRAVEL **2,500** (4,000 km) MILES OVER THE COURSE OF FOUR GENERATIONS. A SINGLE BUTTERFLY TRAVELS AN AVERAGE OF 50 TO 100 MILES (80 to 160 km) **A DAY.**

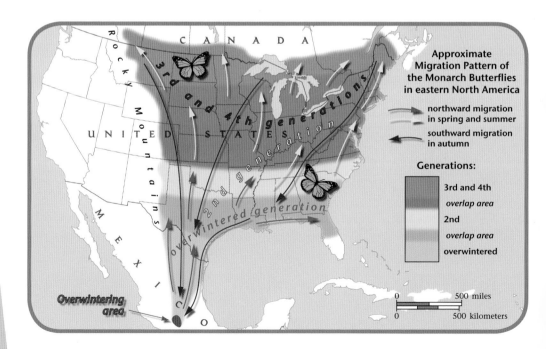

Approximate Migration Pattern of the Monarch Butterflies in eastern North America

northward migration in spring and summer

southward migration in autumn

Generations:

3rd and 4th

overlap area

2nd

overlap area

overwintered

Overwintering area

0   500 miles

0   500 kilometers

MOTIVE TO MOVE:

THE DELICATE BUTTERFLIES CANNOT SURVIVE COLD WINTER TEMPERATURES. IN THE FALL, THEY HEAD SOUTH TO SPEND THE WINTER IN MEXICO. WHEN SPRING ARRIVES, THE BUTTERFLIES TAKE FLIGHT TO THE UNITED STATES AND CANADA WHERE **THEIR FAVORITE FOOD, MILKWEED, IS PLENTIFUL.**

DANGERS:
MONARCHS FACE MANY PREDATORS, BUT THE BUTTERFLIES' **TOXIC SKIN** DISCOURAGES SECOND HELPINGS.

300
MILLION MONARCH BUTTERFLIES FLOCK TO FORESTS IN CENTRAL MEXICO **FOR THE WINTER.**

RELAY RACE

EASTERN MONARCHS CAN'T COMPLETE THEIR ENTIRE JOURNEY within their life span, so the butterflies participate in a multi-generational relay race. Spring's arrival awakens the wintering butterflies in Mexico. They mate and travel north for as little as one month before they die. By instinct, their offspring also know where to go. They continue north, usually reaching the Midwest, where they breed and die. The third generation presses on to the northern United States and Canada.

In the fall, the fourth generation is born. These especially long-lived "super monarchs" make the entire trip back to Mexico themselves. They return to the same forests, sometimes even the same tree, where their great-grandparents started the year before.

JELLYFISH

MILLIONS OF MIGRATING JELLYFISH TRANSFORM AN OTHERWISE ORDINARY LAKE INTO A MAGICAL WORLD OF BOBBING GOLDEN ORBS.

GOLD RUSH

GOLDEN JELLYFISH ARE TRAPPED IN A SALTWATER LAGOON THAT BECAME ISOLATED FROM THE SEA ABOUT 12,000 YEARS AGO.

THE ANIMALS TRAVEL OVER HALF A MILE ACROSS THE LAKE DURING THE DAY, AND TO A DEPTH OF **45 FEET** (13.7 m) EVERY NIGHT.

WITH THE RISE OF THE SUN, SWARMS OF GOLDEN JELLYFISH START A MIGRATION.

While many migrating animals make their move once a year, these jellyfish undertake a major journey every single day. Following the movement of the sun, millions of jellyfish circle the saltwater lake they call home—the appropriately named Jellyfish Lake.

Why does a small, pulsating jellyfish go through all the trouble? Golden jellyfish must follow the sun to support the plant-like algae that grow in their bodies. The algae convert sunlight into sugars for energy. In exchange for protection and a place to live, the algal hitchhikers make extra food for the jellyfish. The algae also give jellyfish their beautiful golden glow.

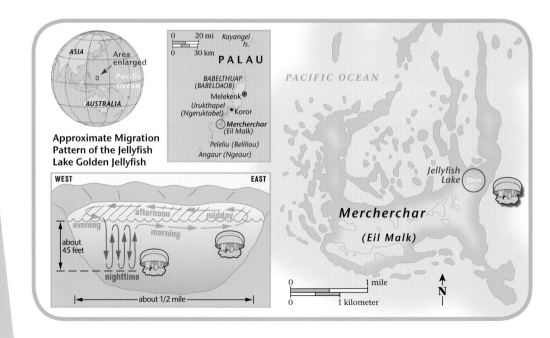

Approximate Migration Pattern of the Jellyfish Lake Golden Jellyfish

ASIA • Area enlarged • *Pacific Ocean* • AUSTRALIA

0 — 20 mi
0 — 30 km
Kayangel Is.

PALAU
BABELTHUAP (BABELDAOB)
Melekeok ⊛
Urukthapel (Ngeruktabel) • Koror
Mercherchar (Eil Malk)
Peleliu (Beliliou)
Angaur (Ngeaur)

PACIFIC OCEAN

Jellyfish Lake

Mercherchar (Eil Malk)

WEST — EAST
afternoon — midday
evening — morning
about 45 feet
nighttime
about 1/2 mile

0 — 1 mile
0 — 1 kilometer
N

MOTIVE TO MOVE:
GOLDEN JELLYFISH MUST MAXIMIZE THEIR TIME IN THE SUN SO THE **ALGAE LIVING IN** THEIR BODIES CAN SURVIVE.

DANGERS:
GOLDEN JELLYFISH HAVE TO AVOID THE SHADE TO KEEP THEIR **ALGAE IN THE SUNSHINE.** STAYING ON THE MOVE ALSO HELPS THE JELLIES AVOID THE **STINGING CLUTCHES** OF A PREDATORY SEA ANEMONE.

10 MILLION GOLDEN JELLYFISH PARTICIPATE IN THIS GREAT MIGRATION.

GENTLE JELLIES

SWIMMING THROUGH A SEA OF JELLYFISH MIGHT SEEM LIKE A PAINFUL IDEA.
But the golden jellies of Jellyfish Lake are famously pain-free swimming companions. Golden jellyfish have stingers, which they use to prey on plankton and other tiny animals. But these stingers aren't strong enough to harm most humans. Snorkeling at Jellyfish Lake is now a popular tourist activity.

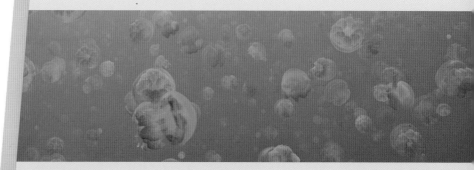

ZEBRAS
PLAYING FOLLOW-THE-LEADER, ZEBRAS COMPLETE THEIR TREK FROM THE DUSTY SAVANNA TO A WELCOME PARADISE OF FRESH GRASS AND WATER.

STRIPED STALLIONS

A ZEBRA'S STRIPES ARE AS UNIQUE AS FINGERPRINTS—NO TWO ARE EXACTLY ALIKE.

THE ANIMALS TRAVEL MORE THAN **1,000** (1,600 km) MILES EACH YEAR.

JUST AS THE AMERICAN WEST HAS ITS MUSTANGS, the Serengeti has

a horse-like animal to call its own: the unmistakable zebra. But zebras don't have time to horse around. Like the region's other hoofed animals—wildebeests and gazelles—zebras must stay on the move for fresh grass and water.

Zebras live in small groups with a dominant male, called a stallion, leading them. Sometimes, herds will come together by the thousands to find better feeding grounds.

Of all Serengeti's grazers, zebras are the least picky. They'll feed on the toughest grasses, paving the way for soft, leafy regrowth that wildebeests and gazelles prefer.

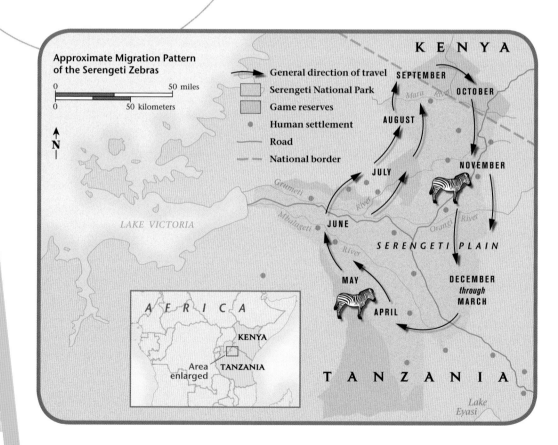

Approximate Migration Pattern of the Serengeti Zebras

0 — 50 miles
0 — 50 kilometers

→ General direction of travel
☐ Serengeti National Park
☐ Game reserves
• Human settlement
— Road
--- National border

KENYA

SEPTEMBER
OCTOBER
AUGUST
NOVEMBER
JULY
JUNE
MAY
APRIL
DECEMBER through MARCH

Mara River
Grumeti
Mbalageti
Orangi River
LAKE VICTORIA
SERENGETI PLAIN

AFRICA
KENYA
Area enlarged TANZANIA

TANZANIA

Lake Eyasi

MOTIVE TO MOVE:

ZEBRAS ARE FOREVER SEARCHING FOR FRESH GRASS AND WATER. THEY FOLLOW ROUGHLY THE SAME MOVEMENTS AS WILDEBEESTS. THE TIMING OF THEIR TRAVELS IS DRIVEN BY RAINFALL, WHICH FUELS THE GROWTH OF **NEW GRASS AND REFILLS WATER HOLES.**

DANGERS:
ZEBRAS MUST ALWAYS BE ON THE LOOKOUT FOR **LIONS, CROCODILES, AND HYENAS.** THE ANIMALS ARE FAVORITE PREY FOR THESE **BIG CARNIVORES.**

ON THE SERENGETI PLAINS, ABOUT

300,000

ZEBRAS PARTICIPATE IN A GREAT MIGRATION.

STRENGTH IN NUMBERS

ZEBRAS HAVE NO SHORTAGE OF ENEMIES ON THE SAVANNA, BUT THEY AREN'T HELPLESS. When a herd is attacked, zebras form a semicircle facing the predator. They're ready to bite or kick an enemy that comes too close.

Zebras' coloring may also help. Perhaps their black-and-white stripes aren't just the Serengeti's boldest fashion statement. It may be that when a predator spots a herd, it sees a jumble of lines, instead of individual zebras. This could mean that as long as zebras stick together, they confuse predators with the play of stripe upon stripe. Or maybe we just don't yet know what role zebras' stripes play on the sunny savanna. Who will solve the mystery of the zebras' stripes?

ARMY ANTS

WITH GIANT HOOKED JAWS, SWARMS OF ARMY ANTS RULE THE RAIN FOREST, FEEDING ON ANYTHING IN THEIR PATH.

DEATH ON THE MARCH

IN COSTA RICA'S CLOUDY RAIN FORESTS, THE KING OF THE JUNGLE ISN'T A BIG CAT. It isn't even a mammal at all. Here, the

army ants rule. All other animals flee for their lives when

they're on the move.

The ants fan out from their home base, heading in a different direction every day for three weeks. The swarm can extend 40 feet (12 m) across and be several hundred feet long. The ants attack in unison, killing and eating anything that lies in their path.

IN RELATION TO THE **ARMY ANT'S** SIZE EACH OF ITS **NIGHTLY MIGRATIONS IS EQUAL TO A HUMAN RUNNING A MARATHON.**

THE ANIMALS TRAVEL ABOUT **6** (10 km) MILES EACH YEAR.

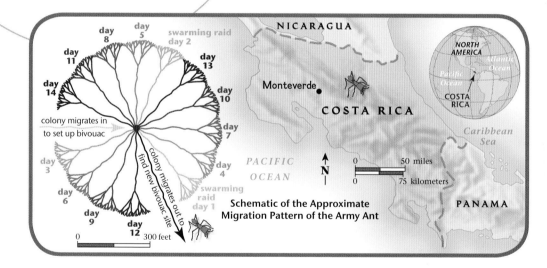

day 8
day 5
swarming raid day 2
day 11
day 13
day 14
day 10
colony migrates in to set up bivouac
day 7
colony migrates out to find new bivouac site
day 3
day 4
day 6
swarming raid day 1
day 9
day 12
0   300 feet

NICARAGUA

NORTH AMERICA
Atlantic Ocean
Pacific Ocean
COSTA RICA

Monteverde
COSTA RICA

Caribbean Sea

PACIFIC OCEAN

N

0   50 miles
0   75 kilometers

PANAMA

Schematic of the Approximate Migration Pattern of the Army Ant

UP TO **1 MILLION** ANTS MAKE UP A **MIGRATING ARMY ANT** COLONY.

MOTIVE TO MOVE:

HUGE COLONIES OF ARMY ANTS MUST TRAVEL DAILY IN ORDER TO FIND ENOUGH FOOD TO SUPPORT THEIR GROWING BROOD. WHEN AN AREA'S FOOD SUPPLY RUNS OUT, **THE ENTIRE COLONY MIGRATES BY NIGHT TO A NEW LOCATION.**

DANGERS:

EVEN THE **LARGEST ARMIES** CAN HAVE **SERIOUS SETBACKS.** SOMETIMES BIRDS SWOOP IN AND **STEAL THE ANTS' MEALS.**

THE ARMY ANT QUEEN IS THE **MOTHER OF THE ENTIRE COLONY.** DURING HER LIFETIME SHE LAYS ABOUT **14 MILLION** EGGS.

INSECT ARMY

IN THE ARMY ANTS' ARMY, EVERY INDIVIDUAL HAS A CLEARLY DEFINED JOB TO DO. The queen and all of the worker ants in the colony are female—males fly away shortly after birth. Soldier workers with long, sabre-shaped jaws protect the colony against predators. Somewhat smaller workers hunt and kill the prey, and cut it into small pieces. Subsoldier workers carry the prey back to the nest. The smallest workers mind the ants' brood of young and care for the queen.

WILDEBEESTS
WHEN THESE BEASTS ARE ON THE MOVE,
THE GROUND TREMBLES BENEATH MILLIONS OF POUNDING HOOVES.

WILD RISKS

WILDEBEESTS TRAVEL IN A ROUGH CIRCLE ACROSS HUGE AREAS OF KENYA AND TANZANIA, A REGION CALLED THE SERENGETI.

THE ANIMALS TRAVEL OVER 1,800 (2,900 km) MILES EACH YEAR.

ON A TANZANIAN PLAIN, A WILDEBEEST IS BORN. ITS MOTHER URGES IT TO STAND.

Human babies can take a year or more to take their first steps. But this young antelope has to be mobile in minutes. In central Africa, it's get up or get eaten!

For a wildebeest, being in a rush is a way of life. That's because they are a favorite snack on the savanna. Lions, leopards, crocodiles, and hyenas all feed on the moving herds. Outrunning enemies means living to see tomorrow. Despite the danger, wildebeests have to follow the seasonal rains to greener grasslands. Water and food are worth braving exhaustion and hungry predators.

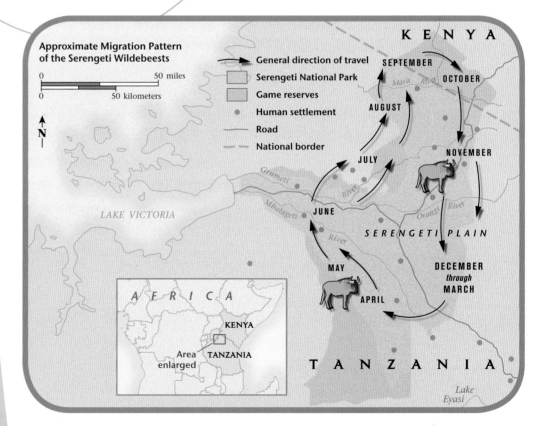

Approximate Migration Pattern of the Serengeti Wildebeests

0 — 50 miles
0 — 50 kilometers

N

- General direction of travel
- Serengeti National Park
- Game reserves
- Human settlement
- Road
- National border

KENYA

SEPTEMBER · OCTOBER · AUGUST · JULY · NOVEMBER · JUNE · MAY · APRIL · DECEMBER through MARCH

Mara River · Grumeti · Mbalageti · Orangi River · River · SERENGETI PLAIN · LAKE VICTORIA

AFRICA · KENYA · Area enlarged · TANZANIA

TANZANIA

Lake Eyasi

MOTIVE TO MOVE:

THE REGION'S ALTERNATING DRY AND RAINY SEASONS MEAN THAT PLANT EATERS HAVE TO STAY ON THE MOVE TO FIND A STEADY SUPPLY OF GREENS. DURING THE DRY SEASONS, THE PLAINS DRY UP INTO BARREN DUST FIELDS. **WILDEBEESTS WOULD STARVE IF THEY DIDN'T MIGRATE.**

DANGERS:

WILDEBEESTS WHO ESCAPE PREDATORS AND SURVIVE THIRST **MAY STILL BE TRAMPLED** IF THEIR HERD IS STARTLED INTO A **FRENZIED STAMPEDE.**

1.4 MILLION

WILDEBEESTS PARTICIPATE IN THIS **GREAT MIGRATION.**

GREEN HOOF-PRINT

THE WILDEBEEST MIGRATION HAS A WIDE IMPACT ON THE LIVES OF PLANTS and animals

across the Serengeti. Heavy grazing by wildebeests stimulates grasses to produce a leafy regrowth. A wildebeest feast means that pickier gazelles can look forward to their favorite ground-clinging herbs and clovers below. Wildebeests also make another—smellier—contribution: Their manure serves as fertilizer for the region's grasslands.

SPERM WHALES THESE GIANTS OF THE SEA
TURN ENTIRE OCEANS INTO THEIR PLAYGROUND.

FAMILY TIES

A SPERM WHALE CAN REACH A LENGTH OF 65 FEET (20 m). IT CAN WEIGH UP TO 45 TONS— THAT'S THE WEIGHT OF 8 MALE ELEPHANTS COMBINED!

FEMALES CAN TRAVEL UP TO 20,000 (32,000 km) MILES A YEAR. A MALE MIGRATES EVEN FARTHER. HE COULD SWIM AROUND THE EARTH 40 TIMES.

PICTURE A YOUNG SPERM WHALE ROLLING

at the water's surface, enjoying a moment of playtime. Its mother is nowhere to be seen, but there are clues to her whereabouts. Bloody chunks of squid pieces float to the surface. They're leftovers from the mother's feast in the depths below. Since the calf isn't ready for these long, dangerous dives, it must wait alone until she resurfaces.

Sperm whales spend their lives searching for enough food to fuel their enormous bodies. Females and their young travel in family groups. They stay in warm, tropical waters throughout the world's oceans. Males cover vast distances, reaching both the Arctic and Antarctic circles. In the fall, some males and females meet at breeding grounds off the Azores Islands, Portugal.

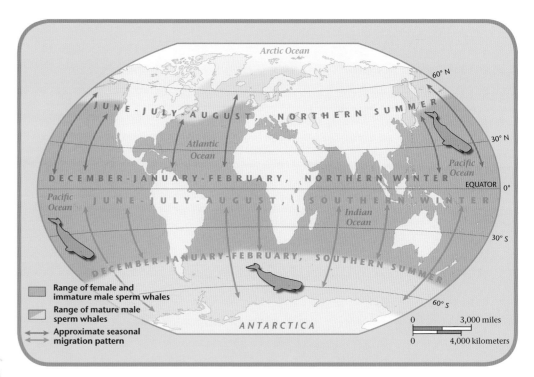

Range of female and immature male sperm whales

Range of mature male sperm whales

Approximate seasonal migration pattern

0 — 3,000 miles

0 — 4,000 kilometers

MOTIVE TO MOVE:

THE SEARCH FOR AREAS WITH PLENTIFUL FOOD AND THE DRIVE TO MATE KEEPS THESE WHALES IN CONSTANT MOTION AROUND THE GLOBE.

NO ONE KNOWS EXACTLY **HOW MANY SPERM WHALES** THERE ARE; AT LEAST **HUNDREDS OF THOUSANDS** ARE THOUGHT TO LIVE IN THE WORLD'S OCEANS.

DANGERS: RUN-INS WITH SHIPS AND GETTING TWISTED IN **FISHING NETS** ARE A SPERM WHALE'S BIGGEST THREATS. ALSO POLLUTION CAN BUILD UP IN THEIR FOOD SOURCES.

THE ANIMALS CAN DIVE UP TO DEPTHS OF **1.5** (2.4 km) MILES AND HOLD THEIR BREATH FOR 1 HOUR AND 13 MINUTES.

LIVING LARGE

SPERM WHALES SEEM TO LIVE IN EXTREMES.

They are the largest toothed animal, the largest living predator, and possess the largest brain of any animal.

An animal of this size must have a big appetite to match. Over a series of long dives, sperm whales gobble up to 700 squid in one day! Scientists have calculated that sperm whales could consume 75 million tons of food from the ocean each year. That's an amount nearly as much as the harvests of all human fisheries combined.

INDEX

Illustrations are indicated by **boldface.**

A

Ants
army ants **32–33**, 34–35, **35**
crazy ants 19
Army ants **32–33**, 34–35, **35**

B

Biodiversity 35
Butterflies **20–21**, 22–23

C

Canada
monarch butterflies **20–21**, 22–23
Christmas Island
red crabs **16–17**, 18–19
Costa Rica
army ants **32–33**, 34–35, **35**
Crabs **16–17**, 18–19
Crazy ants 19

D

Desert animals
elephants **12–13**, 14–15, **15**

E

Elephants **12–13**, 14–15, **15**

F

Food, migrating for
army ants 35
golden jellyfish 26
sperm whales 42, 43

wildebeests 38, 39
zebras 29, 31

G

Golden jellyfish **24–25**, 26–27, **27**
GPS collars 15

I

Insect migrations, longest 21

J

Jellyfish **24–25**, 26–27, **27**

K

Kenya
wildebeests **10–11**, **36–37**, 38–39, **39**
zebras **28–29**, 30–31

M

Mali
elephants **12–13**, 14–15, **15**
Maps
army ant migration 34
elephant migration 14
jellyfish migration 26
monarch butterfly migration 22
red crab migration 18
sperm whale migration 42
wildebeest migration 38
world map of animal migrations 8–9
zebra migration 30

Mating, migrating for
red crabs 18, 19
Mexico
monarch butterflies **20–21**, 22–23
Migration length chart 8
Migration reasons
mating 18, 19
search for food 26, 29, 31, 35, 38, 39, 42, 43
search for water 13, 14, 29, 31, 38
weather 23
Monarch butterflies **20–21**, 22–23
Multigenerational migrations 22, 23

O

Ocean
sperm whales **40–41**, 42–43

P

Palau, Republic of, North Pacific Ocean
golden jellyfish **24–25**, 26–27, **27**

R

Rain forests
army ants **32–33**, 34–35, **35**
biodiversity 35
Red crabs **16–17**, 18–19

S

Sahel (region), Africa
elephants **12–13**, 14–15, **15**
Satellite tracking 15
Serengeti, Kenya-Tanzania
wildebeests **10–11**, **36–37**, 38–39, **39**
zebras **28–29**, 30–31
Sperm whales **40–41**, 42–43

T

Tanzania
wildebeests **10–11**, **36–37**, 38–39, **39**
zebras **28–29**, 30–31

U

United States
monarch butterflies **20–21**, 22–23

W

Water, search for
elephants 13, 14, 15
wildebeests 38
zebras 29, 31
Weather, migrating for
monarch butterflies 23
Whales **40–41**, 42–43
Wildebeests **10–11**, **36–37**, 38–39, **39**

Z

Zebras **28–29**, 30–31

PHOTOGRAPHY CREDITS

Abbreviation Key:
NGS = NationalGeographicStock.com
NGT = National Geographic Television

Cover, (zebras) John Conrad/Corbis; (butterfly) Jim Brandenburg/Minden Pictures/NGS; (whale), Hiroya Minakuchi/Minden Pictures/NGS; (crabs), NGT; (jellyfish), NGT; 2, Anup & Manoj Shah; 3, Anup & Manoj Shah; 5, NGT; 6 (top center), Hiroya Minakuchi/Minden Pictures; 6 (bottom center), NGT; 6 (bottom right), Anup & Manoj Shah; 7 (top left), NGT; 7 (top right), NGT; 7 (bottom center), Anup & Manoj Shah; 10-11, Anup & Manoj Shah; 12-13, Carlton Ward Jr; 16 (center), NGT; 17, NGT; 20 (left), NGT; 20 (right), NGT; 21 (right), NGT; 24, NGT; 25, NGT; 27 (bottom right), NGT; 28-29, Pete Oxford/naturepl.com; 30 (bottom center), Anup & Manoj Shah; 32, Mark Moffett/Minden Pictures/NGS; 33, Christian Ziegler/Minden Pictures/NGS; 35 (bottom right), Mark Moffett/Minden Pictures/NGS; 36 (left), Anup & Manoj Shah; 37 (right), Anup & Manoj Shah; 40-41, Hiroya Minakuchi/Minden Pictures/NGS; 46, NGT; 47, NGT; Back cover, Anup & Manoj Shah

Published by the National Geographic Society

John M. Fahey, Jr., President and Chief Executive Officer
Gilbert M. Grosvenor, Chairman of the Board
Tim T. Kelly, President, Global Media Group
John Q. Griffin, Executive Vice President; President, Publishing
Nina D. Hoffman, Executive Vice President;
    President, Book Publishing Group
Melina Gerosa Bellows, Executive Vice President,
    Children's Publishing

Prepared by the Book Division

Nancy Laties Feresten, Vice President,
    Editor in Chief, Children's Books
Jonathan Halling, Design Director, Children's Publishing
Jennifer Emmett, Executive Editor, Reference and Solo,
    Children's Books
Carl Mehler, Director of Maps
R. Gary Colbert, Production Director
Jennifer A. Thornton, Managing Editor

Staff for This Book

Jennifer Emmett, Project Editor
Eva Absher, Jim Hiscott, and Ruthie Thompson, Art Directors
Lori Epstein, Illustrations Editor
Eva Absher, Designer
Kate Olesin, Editorial Assistant
Sven M. Dolling and Michael McNey, Map Research and Production
Grace Hill, Associate Managing Editor
Lewis R. Bassford, Production Manager
Susan Borke, Legal and Business Affairs

Manufacturing and Quality Management

Christopher A. Liedel, Chief Financial Officer
Phillip L. Schlosser, Vice President
Chris Brown, Technical Director
Nicole Elliott, Manager
Rachel Faulise, Manager

The National Geographic Society is one of the world's
largest nonprofit scientific and educational organizations.
Founded in 1888 to "increase and diffuse geographic
knowledge," the Society works to inspire people to
care about the planet. National Geographic reflects the
world through its magazines, television programs, films,
music and radio, books, DVDs, maps, exhibitions, live
events, school publishing programs, interactive media
and merchandise. National Geographic magazine, the
Society's official journal, published in English and 32
local-language editions, is read by more than 35 million
people each month. The National Geographic Channel
reaches 310 million households in 34 languages in
165 countries. National Geographic Digital Media
receives more than 13 million visitors a month. National
Geographic has funded more than 9,200 scientific
research, conservation and exploration projects and
supports an education program promoting geography
literacy. For more information, visit nationalgeographic.com

For more information, please call 1-800-NGS LINE
(647-5463) or write to the following address:
National Geographic Society
1145 17th Street N.W.
Washington, D.C. 20036-4688 U.S.A.

Visit us online at www.nationalgeographic.com/books

For librarians and teachers: www.ngchildrensbooks.org

More for kids from National Geographic: kids.
nationalgeographic.com

For information about special discounts for bulk
purchases, please contact National Geographic Books
Special Sales: ngspecsales@ngs.org

For rights or permissions inquiries, please contact
National Geographic Books Subsidiary Rights:
ngbookrights@ngs.org

GREAT MIGRATIONS is a global television event from the National Geographic Channel. For more information see www.natgeotv.com/migrations

ACKNOWLEDGMENTS

Special thanks to Dr. Rory Wilson, Department of Pure
and Applied Ecology, Institute of Envrionmental Sus-
tainability, Swansea University, and Dr. Martin Wikel-
ski, Department of Ecology and Evolutionary Biology,
Princeton University, for their review of the text and
layout. Further thanks to Dr. Daniel Kronauer, Harvard
Society of Fellows, Museum of Comparative Zoology Labs,
Cambridge, MA, for his help with the army ant text.

Grateful acknowledgment is given to Nigel R. Franks, Cen-
tre for Behavioural Biology, School of Biological Sciences,
University of Bristol and Iain D. Couzin, Assistant Professor
of Ecology and Evolutionary Biology, Princeton University
for their help with the army ants maps and diagram.

Library of Congress Cataloging-in-Publication Data

Carney, Elizabeth, 1981-
  Great migrations / by Elizabeth Carney. — 1st ed.
     p. cm.
  Includes bibliographical references and index.
  ISBN 978-1-4263-0700-3 (hardcover : alk. paper) —
  ISBN 978-1-4263-0701-0 (library binding : alk. paper)
  1. Animal migration—Juvenile literature. 2. Migratory
animals—Juvenile literature. I. Title.
  QL754.C326 2010
  591.56'8—dc22   2010008501

Scholastic ISBN: 978-1-4263-0811-6

Printed in China
10/RRDS/1